Tea Bags Rise Again!
by Bill Steensland

Chapters

It Starts With a Dream!

Little Billy liked to play with the telephone. Billy was fascinated by the fact that he could hear someone talking to him and talk back even though they were many miles apart. Phones still had rotary dials and long distance calls were very expensive, but when he called a "random" number for a "prank call" the possibilities were endless! There was no worry about getting caught because it was before "caller id." The jokes were silly but fun for a small boy. "Is your refrigerator running? You had better go and catch it!" It was harmless play, but was the seed of what would become one of the great joys of his life and for a time it was his profession!

I am no longer called Billy, but I discovered a grown up version of that child's play when I became a radio talk show host.

This is the story of why I still believe that the combination of a grown up "fun loving" boy, a radio station, and a telephone has been and can be an instrument of great good in our country!

Jesus must have played in the carpenter's shop before he was old enough to work there. Child's play can and often does become man's work. Great mothers play with dolls when they are little girls. Great pianists were once small children who sat at the piano and imagined what it would be like to command respect as a virtuoso!

I want you to join me in doing what may seem to be very silly, but I think it is essential to the future of our country as a free nation. *Imagine that the United States of America has repented and turned back to God.* Pretend that the love of Jesus has become the dominant force in America. Think about what it will be like when Godly morality becomes the expected standard once again across the land. Pretend that men have the freedom to reject God, but not the freedom to force their perspective on everyone else. Imagine that everyone is free to speak of God anytime and anywhere they choose without reprisal. Basically pretend that a Great Revival has swept across this land and restored it. Imagine that Love not Hate is the thing you feel everywhere and that women and children do not have to be afraid to be out alone at night.

Pretend that "truth" is the word for the day and even politicians cannot bring themselves to tell a lie.   The Bible says that if you can think it, God can do it!

So our first job is to:

"THINK ABOUT A RESTORED AND REVIVED 'ONE NATION UNDER GOD.'"

In 1971, John Lennon wrote and recorded a song that encouraged those who have pulled America away from its roots to **Imagine**. They have effectively perverted and stolen the American Dream. The American Dream is not "getting rich and being free." The American Dream is "One Nation Under God, with Liberty and Justice for all."

The song began with the words:

Imagine

Imagine there's no heaven
It's easy if you try
No hell below us
Above us only sky
Imagine all the people
Living for today. . .

Imagine there's no countries
It isn't hard to do
Nothing to kill or die for
And no religion too
Imagine all the people
Living life in peace. . .

For more than 40 years the "fundamental transformation of America" and yes the entire world has been "imagined" by those who are diligently working to bring it about. It is long past time that we also begin to imagine what it will be like when the restoration of America is accomplished.

So let's pretend that someone lights the fire of TURNING BACK TO GOD and back to TRUTH! Imagine that it has spread all across the land and we see nothing but wonderful days ahead.

Now, pray that what you IMAGINE will become REALITY in the United States of America!

America Needs to be Set on Fire!

This little book is the story of what most people believe was just a "Tempest in a teapot." You can judge for yourself, but I believe that October of 1982 was like the moment in time that a great love story began! And I think that much of what is happening today was conceived on "The Bill Steensland Show on WLAC!"

A very wise man once told me how foolish it is to say: "The only thing we can do now is pray!" That is often said after the doctor delivers the report of a terminal illness with no known cure. Prayer is seen as the last resort of those who trusted themselves until they ran out of options. Then they pray!

My wise friend, Robert said that it was like a farmer who wanted to burn down a haystack and after many attempts with wet matches the farmer proclaimed, "The only thing I can do now to light the haystack is to use my blowtorch!"

The United States of America needs to be set on fire! Not a fire of destruction, but a fire of revival toward God. We have tried to light that fire with all the wet matches we have, and it does not work. The only thing we can do now is to pray! So all we have left is the "blow torch" of God's power which we can call upon in prayer.

By the way, there is no "power" in prayer. Prayer does not do anything except call on the One who has all the power. If you pray for someone to be healed and they get well it is not your prayer that did it. It was God!

Rip Van Winkle

Frankly, I feel like Rip Van Winkle who fell asleep one day and woke up 20 years later. Only for me it was more than 30 years ago when I closed my eyes. It was 1982 and Ronald Reagan was President. He warned that "government" was not the solution to the problem. He said "Government is the problem!" When the TEA BAG Campaign (mailing tea bags to congressional leaders as a protest to taxes and excessive spending) was born in that year we saw that the desire to be free and unburdened by overbearing government regulation and taxes was very much alive and well. President Reagan stood strong for individual liberties and he called out Evil in the world. I specifically remember deciding that with President Reagan in the White House "everything will be OK!" Then I dozed off and slept soundly through the Bush-Clinton-Bush Presidencies. Then with the coming of B.H. Obama I began to wake up and realize that while I was sleeping the world was changing around me, and not for the better.

I write this in hopes that history will not repeat itself and we go back to sleep while the Progressive movement completes its dastardly deed! The TEA BAG mail in campaign in 1982 was an "awakening," but then we were lulled back to virtual unconsciousness. The TEA PARTY movement of 2009 was another awakening. The danger now is that we go back to sleep, and this time it may be a sleep from which we will not awaken! We must not, cannot rest until the *culture of freedom* in a "God fearing" country is revived and firmly placed once again on the heart of every American!

In these pages you will find some "hard facts" and some things that I am sure I "remember" correctly. But I am now in my 60's, so you know that some of what I remember is polished by the passage of time. Anything that I have remembered incorrectly, I apologize for the error. But please don't throw out the message of this book because of a factual error from the memory of a *now old* man.

Finally, I ask you to forgive my "rabbit trail writing." I write like I talk and staying too tightly tied to one subject without exploring other areas as they come up takes away a lot of the fun! So please enjoy and trust that I will tie it all together in the end!

How it all began

It wasn't my idea. A lady in Bastrop, Texas called my radio talk show on WLAC in October of 1982. She said something like: "*I'm so upset about taxes. I'm going to send a TEA BAG to Congress!*" Of course, she was wanting to resurrect the message of the Boston Tea Party and apply that sentiment to the "tax and spend" issues of the United States Government. It sounded like a good idea, so I suggested that she send one tea bag to Senate Majority Leader, Howard Baker and one to Speaker of the House, Tip O'Neill. That one phone call morphed into a six week, 28 state marathon of pledges for tea bags and produced a seed that took another 25 years to sprout and begin to cover the land. I believe that today's Tea Party Movement came from that same soil.

WLAC at night covered 28 of our 50 states. It was before the days of the Internet and email. We didn't even have an 800 number, so all the callers had to pay long distance charges for their time on the air. In order to save them some money and to make the show more spontaneous I stopped screening calls. The first words they heard when I answered the phone were "*Hello you are live on WLAC.*" We did have a six second delay, but rarely used it because the level of public obscenity seems to have been a lot lower than it is today.

In those days the "Fairness Doctrine" was still in effect and we were under the obligation to see that both sides of an issue were presented in the course of the program. Frankly, I didn't see that as a hindrance. What we had during those shows was a great contest of ideas. Today we have "pep rallies." Then, there was active conflict on the issues, today we simply talk about how stupid the other side is for not agreeing with us! Pep rallies are OK, but when you play the game, you score some points and the other side scores as well. In the end the winner is declared and there can be a genuine victory celebration! I don't think "one sided" talk shows serve us well as a people. That is an issue worth looking at in more depth.

I was in my mid thirty's when the TEA BAG campaign dominated my nightly talk show on WLAC, a 50,000 watt AM station in Nashville, Tennessee. I remember a caller who snidely asked if I was old enough to do a talk show. I responded that I was old enough to be the President of the United States. He didn't ask if I was smart enough to be the President. That answer would have been "no," or perhaps "I am smart enough not to even consider being the President." I think I still have a copy of a letter that was sent by one of the "loyal" listeners. She said the answer to our problems as a country would be for me to run for President. What she didn't know, but we all know now is that having a President who is not qualified and has very little experience means nothing but trouble for our country.

If you would like to hear a sample of what happened during those days there is a short YouTube video of some of the highlights. Search YouTube for Tea Bag - WLAC - Bill Steensland or click on this link. (http://youtu.be/qxXmeWWtgBE) To give you some perspective I am a few years older than Rush Limbaugh, he did a news commentary on a local station in Kansas City when

I was the drive time talk show host on Kansas City's KCMO. I never met Rush but I do understand what he is doing and the secret of his success. He is doing a show that touches the heart of how Talk Radio should work.

Let me give you one more example from the golden days of controversial talk radio. My personal goal was to have callers who strongly disagreed with my point of view. If you are a listener to a talk show where the host and a caller are having a strong argument you cannot turn it off until one side has prevailed over the other. And it was important that sometimes I would be the one who would lose the argument. If I always won, adventuresome and brave souls would not call and much of the excitement of the contest was greatly diminished. And by the way, no one talked over someone else on my shows. It has become common and I suppose thought to be exciting that two guests or even the guest and the host both talk at once. And when they do that it is usually a very animated presentation by both. The problem is, of course that no one can hear either side of the argument. That kind of noise is truly annoying and not instructive. No one learns anything, and all it displays is the ignorance of those involved. I had the upper hand since I had the microphone controls. If you wanted to talk over me, I would simply turn you down. And if I "needed" to politely interrupt your "rant" I could turn you off and insert my own perspective. I only used the "dump button" on serious violators, with one exception.

During a rather non-threatening discussion one night, my mother called the show. My mother loved to talk and I certainly did learn the art of telephone conversation by listening to her when I was a small child. But my mother, like all of us sometimes do said something that night I knew she would later regret. So, I quickly decided she really wouldn't want what she said on the air, so I used the "dump button" and disconnected the call! Of course, I called her back during the next commercial break to ask her forgiveness and she thanked me for disconnecting her call before her statement could be heard. But among the other talk show hosts at WLAC I got the reputation of being so tough on the air that I would "dump" my own mother!

Again, using tea bags as the medium of expressing our dissatisfaction with Congress came from a lady in Bastrop, Texas! I like the word Bastrop and wish it could be used to identify the whole concept of protesting government over taxation and excessive spending. Perhaps we should call it "The Bastrop Syndrome!" How about a bumper sticker that says "Remember the lady from BASTROP!"

I was not the father of the protest, but perhaps I could be credited with delivering the "baby!"

It Gave Us Something to do!

Even thirty years ago the ills of our nation seemed critical if not terminal. I remember my grandmother telling me that politicians are almost always liars. When an honest man was elected to public office his transition into a "traditional politician" was usually fairly swift.

Sending Tea Bags to politicians may seem almost irrelevant, but it really was a clear and significant statement by those who have "had enough." We encouraged the bags to be sent without any note of explanation. Thousands of people trying to explain why they are protesting is confusing, but hundreds of thousands of "used" tea bags gives a distinct message. In essence without the notes all the messages are the same as they quietly put the elected leaders of our country on notice that the clock has run out!

When multitudes of people raise their voices in protest to their leaders by doing many different things the effect of the protest is diluted. But when one thing is the vehicle of protest it becomes amazingly strong and even frightening. When that one thing is anonymously delivering a tea bag to our leaders the prospect of retaliation is low.

1982 was prior to the days of international terrorism and mail showed up without serious screening efforts. Today the flow of tea bags would be stopped at a hidden screening room and they would probably never be seen by the leaders for whom they were intended. It is just one of the problems of living in a post 911 world. There are ways around the problem and we will discuss them later.

It was just a few months ago that one of the WLAC listeners found me on Facebook and sent me a "message." He told me how much my talk show of the early 1980's meant to him and he just wanted me to know that. I was frankly stunned that someone would still remember what we did these many years later.

Nothing changed as far as our government was concerned because of the Tea Bag campaign, but something did change in many people who listened and sent the Tea Bags to Washington. The thing that changed was that we came to believe that we could speak loudly to our leaders and that our "loud voice" would be heard! I think the thing that stopped the Tea Bag Campaign from growing was the President himself. When Ronald Reagan became President we all began to believe that he would stand up to the "liberals" just as he did to the Soviet Union and that we would not have to keep shouting from the sidelines. But by the time President Reagan left office we were being told to "read my lips" and that a tax increase would be as likely as a coupe in the White House. There was a tax increase and many believe there was a "coupe in the White House," with the election of William Jefferson Clinton. (No, I will not explain that assertion in this book!)

As a Presidential Candidate, Barack Obama declared that he would fundamentally transform America. We all now know that he was not "just talking." From his first day in office he set about to "make good" on the radical changes that have been desired by liberals, socialists, and even communists for many years.

As we are seeing in other countries around the world, sometimes nothing will change until the voice of the people is so loud that the leaders can hear nothing else. For many years we have declared that change in America must come about by the use of ballots, not bullets! I do not believe we are at the point where bullets would be necessary, but with the use of "social media" and electronic voting "irregularities" I believe we have arrived at a time for the persistent, public, and perpetual expression of dissatisfaction with our government not simply voting! The Federal Government is now listening to us in every place – possibly even monitoring this as I write – so they need to come to the conclusion that the opposition is not a "vast right wing conspiracy" but indeed the opposition is a "vast reality."

Remember the Jews who quietly let Hitler reduce their freedoms until he took away their freedom to live. If you think that could never happen here remember that we have already expressed support for "rebels" in Syria who cannibalized a Syrian soldier and decapitated a Catholic Priest with a kitchen knife! And we seem to sit quietly by as ISIS decapitates Americans and lets us see the videos on You Tube!

As the Tea Bag mail in progressed, there were a few other things that happened on the WLAC show. Larry King followed my show on WLAC with his national radio show. I frequently listened to some of Larry's show while on my way home from work. We scheduled a brief live interview with Larry King one night shortly before the end of the shift. After an opening greeting and little chit chat I opened the phone lines and a caller said "Larry did you know that Bill Steensland is the guy behind the Tea Bag Campaign?"

Larry went on a little rampage about the Tea Bag Campaign. To the best of my memory he declared that it was "stupid" and wouldn't accomplish anything. Instead of arguing with Larry King, which I suppose I should have done, I was polite and ended the interview as quickly as possible. I did not hang up on Larry King, but I was indeed tempted to do so. Larry knew about the Tea Bag Campaign because many of my faithful callers also called Larry's show and told him

about it.

Perception Principle

I think a chapter about a Bible Story would be appropriate in any good book. So let's include the story of Gideon in this one.

Gideon is the story of a man who despite his humble beginnings was able to defeat an overwhelming enemy with only 300 soldiers. The army of Midian was camped and ready to overrun Israel. God chose Gideon to lead His army against the mighty foe. Thousands of volunteers were culled down to 300 men with trumpets and torches. When the trumpets blew and torches became visible the Midianite army panicked and ran away in fear.

There were only 300 men, but these few soldiers stood with the authority and power of God behind them. The victory was won in the minds of the enemy. The sweetest conquest is when truth and the righteousness of God drive away the enemy without a single shot being fired!

There is much talk today about the Constitutional right to "bear arms." But remember the best victory comes when the enemy runs away because you are obviously better armed than they are and then fear causes them to panic.

I think "righteous intimidation" is a good thing. If you saw God Almighty standing on one side and Satan on the other which one would be more frightening? Clearly God is the most Awesome Being and He overwhelms every sense that we have.

Even if we are fighting a well armed military force, the victory will come to those who like Gideon are obedient to God and listen to His Word!

What can Modern Day Patriots in the United States learn from the story of Gideon? We tell ourselves that the victory is all about numbers. When a nation is threatened like the United States has been and is being threatened it is much more about the CHARACTER of the Patriots and not the QUANTITY! One George Washington is worth more than a million complacent soldiers. Are we wanting to simply restore the economic strength of our land or do we desire that this nation be restored to "One Nation Under God" in it's truest sense? If the revolution is about "getting back the goodies" then we cannot expect the blessings of God. If the movement is about personal revival and honoring God as a nation, then there is hope that we may even be greater than we have ever been.

I believe that a significant turn away from God took place in the 1930's and 40's. Check out Netflix and watch a few movies from that era and see if you find God honored or even mentioned in most of the productions. Perhaps it wasn't a very ungodly period of our history, but it was a very "godless" time. Personal faith was rarely depicted in those productions.

And certainly, in the 1950's and 60's the "good times rolled" and we became religious, but not devoted to Jesus. I don't believe that going back to those days will bring us anything that we are looking for. We need to be "reborn" with revival and re-dedication flooding over this land.

There needs to be a Gideon who hears the call of God and rises up to defeat the enemy with power of God clearly supporting his every move! Gideon may already be among us. Only time will tell if he is the one to lead us to victory over those who desire our downfall!

Car Without an Engine

I am looking for a new car. Well of course it is a new-old car that I need. New cars are way beyond making sense for my pocket book. I saw a beautiful car on line that was just the right year and everything. Even the price was right, but when I read the small print I discovered that it had no engine! Of course, a car with no engine would not be useful.

America is looking for a way to drive out of our serious predicaments. But she is trying to drive a car with no engine. The engine that has driven America to the top of world over these past 200 plus years is faith in God. IN GOD WE TRUST is not just a saying. It is the engine that has driven this nation for more than two centuries. So the solution to our problems is simple. All we have to do is restore our faith and trust in God and the Ship of State will begin to steam out of these troubled waters. If we refuse to cry out to God as a nation then we like Humpty Dumpty will be doomed to become a story that has an end, and not a very pretty one at that. When "all the king's horses and all the king's men" tried to put Humpty Dumpty back together again they failed.

We were a nation running on power that came from on High! We fashioned our laws from Biblical truths and we had a morality that paralleled the ethics of the New Testament and we prospered in material things! That's when we began to turn away from God. It has been slow, but steadily and almost without exception every year takes us closer to the total abandonment of God.

We foolishly have declared that our freedom has come from "Democracy". If people can have "free" and honest elections then they too will prosper like the USA! Freedom does not come from Democracy or free and honest elections. Freedom comes from our Creator not from any philosophy of government. When men and women who have been set free by God come together to form a government, that government will be free and provide freedom to it's citizens. When men and women who are enslaved by sin form a government, that government will simply reflect the slavery of it's founders!

I want to declare that all the efforts we make to restore our Republic without our hearts being first restored to God will fail and fail badly! Making cosmetic changes to the externals of this nation will not give it the power to move forward! Which would you rather have, a rather worn and even a little rusted car with a perfect engine and drive train, or a beautiful car with a dead power plant? Let us focus on the power behind our success as a nation and invite God back into our Government!

Take a Stand

Are you afraid to take a stand on the issues that threaten your life or the welfare of our country today? That fear of standing firm, of course comes from the "possible consequences" of saying no to those who want to exchange the truth for a lie. There are always consequences of holding on to truth. If you decide to stand up against an attack dog, you may win the fight, but undoubtedly you will be injured in the process.

While a radio talk show host at WHBQ in Memphis the city government decided to outlaw "topless dancing". The problem was, as I remember it, the law would apply to bars and clubs, but not to the opera. The local performing theater had booked a live opera in Memphis which included at least one topless performer. The new law would not apply to an opera. After I uncovered and talked about the hypocrisy (no pun intended), I became very unpopular among those who were able and apt to go to the opera. One of the club dancers called my show and said she wanted to get out of the business but could not afford to make the change. Memphis is a city of many churches. So I spent the balance of that show asking for someone to come forward and offer to help her in supporting her daughter with another job. No one called! That still upsets me today when I think about it. I have regretted that I didn't do more in getting her connected with the assistance she wanted. I know that now there are those who offer to help and to minister to women caught in that world, but society in general then just wanted to condemn, not help.

The abortion issue is still taboo for many talkers. One woman called to argue that it was "a woman's right to choose." I simply asked if there was a point at which the baby's right to live took over. She seemed confused by the question. I said how about a month before the baby is born, could the baby have the right to live at that point? She responded that a month before birth would be OK. Then I suggested a week. She agreed. She also agreed that the baby could be given the "right to life" just a few seconds before a live birth. Then I said why not give the woman another three months after the baby is born to decide whether or not to let the baby live! Believe it or not the woman agreed! I closed out the conversation and told her that I was very glad that she was not my mother!

Sometimes you need "wisdom from above" when you take a stand and engage the "intelligentsia." A man who sounded like a professor made an opening statement and then declared with great certainty "There is no such thing as an absolute." With what I am sure was an infusion of Godly wisdom I responded "Are you absolutely sure?" That ended the conversation!

When you take a stand today there will be three possible outcomes. You may be ignored altogether. You may be ridiculed and embarrassed or you may light the fire of positive change in the world around you. If you fear being ignored, ridiculed and embarrassed then you forfeit the possibility of being one of those who makes a difference.

1982 was also the year of the Bloomington baby, who came to be known as Baby Doe. A Down Syndrome baby was left to die of starvation and thirst because the baby had Down Syndrome and needed a simple surgery. It was already 9 pm when a caller from Indiana called my show and asked for help. I had no idea when the call first came in how far this would go. It was an extremely emotional time. Someone suggested that we send telegrams to President Reagan. It was before the day of email, fax and social media. We encouraged that the message simply be "Save the Bloomington baby!" I specifically asked that no mention be made of my talk show. People called from more than 20 states pledging to send that message to President Reagan. The effort came too late for Baby Doe, but the Federal Government did subsequently discourage the practice of starving Down Syndrome babies. I believe it was at least partly as a result of my talk show audience's response.

In recent years there has been the suspicion that voter fraud and manipulation has been a serious problem. There are those who want to swell the vote count in an election with undocumented aliens and absentee votes by dead people. For some strange reason we don't take the problem seriously. I frankly think we should consider voter fraud to be as serious as Treason, because indeed it is! Voter fraud is manipulating the foundation of our nation. It can change the direction of the nation for generations to come. I believe voter fraud is a greater crime than giving away our secrets. Perhaps the penalty for voter fraud should include losing your US citizenship and then deportation. Have we no understanding that to have the outcome of one national election changed because of voter fraud permanently changes our history and national life! It must not be tolerated at any level.

How much of our government now is bogus because of illegal voter fraud? There is a strange belief that even if someone got into office illegally, that once they are there, nothing can be done. It seems we deal with illegal voting like we deal with illegal immigration. We throw up our hands and just hope it will stop if we ignore it long enough. Voter fraud is the same as attempting to overthrow our government by force. The man in Cleveland who imprisoned three girls for ten years did not get exonerated because he was not caught for many years. There should be no "statute of limitation" on voter fraud! There should be no election that stands with "significant" allegations of voter fraud unresolved.

Whether or not our President was born in the United States is not an insignificant issue. If it is determined by factual evidence that our President was not qualified to serve Constitutionally in that office then he should be removed and retroactively erased from the record! I believe that should be the case whether he is Republican, Democrat, Libertarian or Whig! To make that issue a joke or a conspiracy theory is beyond foolish. Now please don't misunderstand I am not and will not be a "BIRTHER." But factual evidence must be presented to establish the eligibility of a man or woman to become President of the United States. I have not heard that the evidence is there in an undisputed form for our current President.

Organization

What is the difference in sending a Tea Bag and joining an organization? The difference is simple, but I think it is also profoundly important. This is not to say that Tea Party organizations aren't significant. They certainly can play an important role is the helping to make the changes that need to come. But if only those people who join an organization will be effective in implementing change, it will not likely happen.

If you wanted to get rid of all the "Knock Knock" jokes in this country how would you do it? Well, let's see! Who tells those jokes and where do they tell them? Comedians tell jokes and they tell them in Comedy Clubs. So if you want to get rid of "Knock Knock" jokes, make it illegal for comedians to tell them and then close down the comedy clubs as well. Would that work? Of course it wouldn't work because all kinds of people tell "Knock Knock" jokes, and they tell them everywhere!

Tea Party organizations are just that, organizations. They are legal entities that even have attempted to get tax exempt status from the government. In short, organizations are easy targets. The Tea Parties were not significant players in the 2012 Presidential election. We now know that many, if not most of them were tied up with the IRS and were certainly not working at full strength.

"Tea Bags" can be delivered anonymously. The only harm they do, and this was a rumor that came from Senator Howard Baker's office, is that they are really hard on office shredders. And if they are used and not completely dried then the mess is multiplied. But, how do you retaliate against a mountain of used tea bags? I suppose if the campaign went on long enough we would have seen a new law prohibiting the mailing any kind of symbolic protest substance to Congress. I think undoubtedly the mailing of Tea Bags is not the way to do it today. But it must be something else which is just as effective and annoying!

History repeats itself! That concept is usually used to refer to bad things happening over and over again because we don't learn lessons from past mistakes.

But History can repeat itself in a positive way as well. Men will rise up and oppose the evil and oppressive king when it becomes clear that nothing else will stop him. Revolutions and cultural purges come after a growing number of the people reach a zero tolerance level for the oppression of government in the lives of the governed. Men with the moral underpinning of faith in God will stand as Gideon's soldiers did and blow the trumpet and let their light shine for the enemy to see!

One Thing!

E pluribus unum – these words are included on the Seal of the United States. "One from many" originally referred to one nation from many states. Later it came to mean one nation from many peoples around the world. I want to respectfully suggest that "E pluribus unum" be used to rescue this nation from the pit of Hell into which we are descending.

There are many, many things going on today which are designed to remind us of our heritage and draw us back to our roots. Groups and individual voices can be heard all over the land. What is needed now is that "one thing" comes from the many – we need a new E PLURIBUS UNUM!

If my house is sitting on one acre of ground and a rain storm drops one inch of rain then I have just received 27,154 gallons of water! If that same amount of water drops only on my "old white house" which is thirty feet by thirty feet, then I have received 48.4 inches of rain! The key to making a memorable impact and lasting change is to come together and do ONE THING – not many things! One inch of rain falling on your house will never be remembered, but 48.4 inches of rain will never be forgotten! E Pluribus Unum – from many ideas and actions of concern and protest we need to focus on ONE THING. The people of Egypt who wanted to change their government did ONE THING. They went out into the streets and stayed there until the change was made.

What is the ONE THING that Americans need to do to turn back the clock and restore the US to a place where the system worked? Like a computer that is locked up and unable to function we must restore our "operating system" to a time when it worked. It is not working now, and will not work with the viruses of progressivism and socialism crowding out and even dismantling capitalism.

I wish I could say "Here is the ONE THING that we need to all do to turn it around!" If I knew I certainly would say it. But I cannot know that until we come together on that ONE THING. While we still do many things to address the overwhelming decline of the United States we will continue to be only an annoyance to those who want to fundamentally transform America.

Give Them a Call!

One possibility of presenting our leaders with a VIRTUAL TEA BAG would be to go to the phones instead of the streets. If the public phone lines into the White House and Congress were always filled with callers who simply said "I would like to deliver a virtual tea bag to the President and Congress" the impact could be significant.

The ONE THING must become a rallying point even as sitting in non acceptable places on buses and at lunch counters became the earmark of the Civil Rights Movement.

One night on WLAC a "regular" and somewhat annoying caller popped up on the phones as he usually did maybe once in a three hour show. In the spirit of having fun after I quickly said goodbye to John (that is not his real name) and put him on hold instead of hanging up the phone. Then when I said "Hello you are live on WLAC" there he was again. He began his "annoying" remarks again and I did the same thing. So John was on that night four or five times in a row. It appeared that he had found a way to dominate my phone line.

I don't think I ever did that again and I did have a twinge of guilt for not being totally honest with the audience about what was going on, but it helped me realize how upsetting it can be to have your phone line clogged up with one issue callers.

Never forget that freedom of speech does not mean that the listener will want to hear what you have to say. In fact, the listener may do everything in his power not to hear what you are saying. And you have the freedom to speak louder and in many places. Our freedom of speech is not just the freedom to whisper! Of course you do not have the right to yell "fire" in a crowded theater, unless there is a fire, but you do have the right to speak loudly enough to be heard above the background noise of this world.

Speaking is indeed a form of warfare. The freedom of speech which is guaranteed in the Constitution of the United States means that we have the right to wage war with words. I have the right to ignore what you say, but in the United States you have the right to say it! A wise college professor once told me that "you never learn anything from someone with whom you agree!"

The goal of waging war with words is not to destroy your opponent. The goal is to come together with him on the platform called TRUTH. I don't need to be afraid of TRUTH, even if that TRUTH contradicts things that I have believed. TRUTH is the standard under which all men can come together.

I used to say "Truth is like a boat with no holes in it. It doesn't matter how you throw it in the water. A boat with no holes will always float."

Whatever the ONE THING is, it must be simple, easy for anyone to do, and ultimately very annoying! At first our politicians, including the President will ignore it. Then they will make fun of it! Then they will declare that they understand the point and that we should quit! Finally they will lash out in desperation and declare that we are breaking a new law that they just made up!

The best way for the story to end is for those in power to ultimately get the point and Read the Tea Leaves! Then they must make the changes that need to be made to restore us to our rightful place in the world. But never forget that unless we turn back to the One whose moral principles are the underpinnings of our country nothing else we do will succeed!

An Actor in the White House

When Ronald Reagan first ran for the Presidency I was not at all impressed. Actors are skilled at pretending to be someone that they are not. It is difficult enough to know the heart of any man running for the highest office in the land, but I thought it would be impossible with an actor in pursuit of the White House. My opinion of Ronald Reagan changed dramatically over the next eight years, as did the opinion of many of the American people. This "B" rated movie star was a triple "A" President!

When a guest for your talk show arrives at the station early, it is not a problem unless the guest is one week early! I was in my final few minutes of preparation one night on WLAC when Hollywood actor Keenan Wynn showed up a week early for a guest appearance. If you don't know Keenan Wynn by name you would certainly recognize his face. He appeared in scores of movies. My calendar said he was to come the next week, but there he was and ready to for the interview. I quickly rescheduled the guest who was already there.

His appearance that night gave me some very good insight into why it might be better to have a "B" rated actor in the White House than a really good one. When I asked him about his famous Vaudeville performer, father, Ed Wynn, Keenan showed little interest in talking about it. But when I asked him about the art of acting all of his lights turned on bright and we were off and running. Keenan said that he had appeared in many mediocre movies and shows, but that he had never done a mediocre job of acting. It was his passion. Then there was one of my most memorable "talk show moments." When I asked Keenan Wynn if actors put water drops in their eyes to make it look like they were crying he said, "No, at least for me, they are real." Then he proceeded to produce real tears while I watched. It is still hard for me to believe, but I do remember seeing it myself.

Keenan Wynn taught me that the impassioned speeches of politicians may or may not represent the content of their hearts, much less their character! Human beings have the capability to be "great pretenders" who can, like the Pied Piper lead the children astray. While children play with their toys the politicians lead them to give up the freedoms that were won with the blood of brave Americans over the course of our history.

When the continuing history of the United States is written, our chapter will either be a watershed going down to the final loss of liberty or it will tell about the rebirth of American freedom! If we are wise enough to give up on the "false promises" of a government that lulls us to sleep and then steals our freedoms we may indeed be able to turn the Ship of State around. But if we follow the "pretenders" who fill our ears with nothing but beautiful words while their deeds are ugly and some say "evil" we will end up on the rocky shoreline of history with all the other Great Nations who lost their way and sailed into the rocks!

A Word about the Boston Tea Party

There was a 1973 tea bag "mail in" which is mentioned in <u>Radicals for Capitalism</u> "A Freewheeling History of the American Libertarian Movement" by Brian Doherty. He says ". . between 1972 and 1976, a lot of political energy went into **wan** stunts like celebrating the two-hundredth anniversary of the Boston Tea Party by mailing tea bags to politicians and milling around in front of IRS offices on April 15." According to my dictionary the word "wan" means, "lacking in forcefulness, competence, or effectiveness."

So the idea of mailing tea bags to congress was not original in 1982, but it was done for a completely different reason. It was not done in memory of the Boston Tea Party, but rather to look forward to and hopefully set up the next American Revolution. The goal was that this one would be fought with ballots and not bullets!

It is quite interesting that the tea was dumped in Boston Harbor not because the tax was too high. It was thrown overboard because the colonies were not represented in the government of England and consequently had no say in the matter. It was the same conflict that we still have today when our President issues executive orders that supersede the Congress or the will of the people.

Will we give our freedoms to those who want to steal them, or will we stand up to the tyrants and re-establish this government, *by, for and of the people*?

A Word About the Title

I don't want you to misunderstand the title of this book. TEA BAGS RISE AGAIN, The Second Coming of a Movement.

The Second Coming and the Resurrection of Jesus Christ are not to be made profane. But they do teach a very important lesson which I believe is applicable to what is going on in the United States. When the TEA BAGS came the first time many of us expected that things would change. They did not! When the concept of the TEA BAGS - Tea Party came the second time in 2009 we were given another opportunity and this time the movement grew mightily. The Tea Parties were attacked viciously by the IRS in 2012 prior to the Election, but the movement survived. The 1982 Tea Bag Campaign was an early sign of the anti-tax and overspending sentiment that went dormant, but has come back a second time.

The United Sates of America is a nation which prints "In God We Trust" on their money but now works diligently to exclude God from our government and the lives of it's people.

Unless we begin again to recognize God and trust Him in each area of our government and national life, there is really no way out of our predicament. So if you are reading this and thinking because of the title that it is a "religious" book, then you are wrong, but you are also right! A nation that is blessed when it declares itself under His care will not continue to enjoy those blessings after it declares itself free from the influence of God!

How a Radio Talk Show Works!

In some ways we have ignored the power of a talk radio to help us accomplish the goal. A radio talk show is not what it seems! There are callers and there are listeners. The novice talk show host is very tempted to do the show for the pleasure of the callers. That will make only a few people happy. I learned to do the show for the listeners, not the callers. The goal of the show was always to maximize the listeners and use the callers to create an atmosphere that is irresistible to those who would only listen. If every caller is happy with the show, then you know you have at least a dozen or so happy people listening! If every caller is furious about what is going on, you know you have is a good sized and growing percentage of the available audience. There is a strong temptation to solicit callers who want to say that you are right about everything and are wonderful in every way. A show with those callers will only touch a limited number of people.

The last night that I was on WLAC in Nashville, a man called who said, "I have listened to you three hours a night, five nights a week for two years and I have never ever agreed with anything you ever said!" I responded with, "You have just given me the greatest complement I have ever received."

You can be "a rascal" just to get ratings, but that is just the other side of the coin on trying to make everybody like you. Neither one will work. The answer is to hold on to the TRUTH and go with TRUTH no matter what the reaction. When truth is the pursuit there will be some who love what you are doing and many who hate it. The man who was my best coach in TALK RADIO once told me, "When you get a letter of praise. Ignore it! But when you get a letter of criticism ask yourself if there is any truth in it. If there is, then make the appropriate adjustments." He said if you believe the praise, it will be your downfall!

Here is perhaps the most important secret. When I was on the air I fully believed that I only had one listener. That was it. In my mind, there was never a huge audience of people. So I was about as nervous as I would be talking to a stranger on the telephone. It really wasn't a mind game because people do listen to radio by themselves. If there are two or three people together they are usually talking and the radio is only background noise. I have never heard of a large group of people gathered around a radio (at least in the United States) listening to a talk show! And I never forgot that at any moment there might be no one listening, except my father. I think he always listened!

Conservative talk radio used to be a place where minds were changed because the issues were honestly debated. When "TRUTH" is the platform on which the debate is held minds are changed in both directions. Some conservative positions are not supported by factual evidence and of course some; perhaps many liberal positions have erroneous foundations. When the restrictions of the Fairness Doctrine were removed the "blessing" turned out to be a curse. It would be like your mother saying, "You don't have to eat your vegetables any more. It is just desert and candy for you!"

The traditional conservative (Southern) position on race in this country was not based on truth. Any way you look at it, the "old south" was not honorable or godly about how it dealt with people who had brown skin! The first speech I ever heard from the lips of B.H. Obama was in the wake of the Jeremiah Wright controversy. He spoke much truth in that speech and I was deeply moved. I sincerely hoped that his positions on other things were on target. They were not and he has even proved to be unreliable as a witness about matters of race. I grew up in the south and know from experience that racism is not dead. I think it is very sad that those who were mistreated so badly for years because of the color of their skin are now doing the same thing to anyone pulled into their web of deceit. George Zimmerman is not my hero, but he is not a racist! What we are hearing from the sons and daughters of those who won the honorable civil rights battle is truly pathetic and a disgrace to their cause.

A radio talk show host is something like a man carrying a concealed weapon! It can be used for great good, or it can be tool of great evil! It is only when TRUTH itself is the

focal point of the show that no harm will come to honorable

men and women. The other motives like SUCCESS,

MONEY, FAME, etc. will ultimately bring pain and defeat.

How I Got in the Business

It is very likely that you have never heard of Bill Steensland or my talk radio programs in the early 1980's. That was a long time ago and we were testing the water for what would become a nationwide phenomenon.

How it got started for me was simple. In October of 1980 WLAC in Nashville, Tennessee switched to an "all talk" format and imported a couple of "Big Guns" to fill the prime time slots. Neil Rogers and Charles Cappas were skilled and controversial, but definitely not conservative. Neil Rogers only stayed at WLAC for one month. Both Rogers and Cappas were comfortable debating conservative issues, but they avoided engaging anyone who wanted to talk about what the Bible says. Nashville is in the heart of the Bible Belt in this country and many callers liked to reference their faith in the course of their call. It did become a problem. Neil Rogers would respond to comments about the Bible, but he said he was an atheist and a homosexual, so the conversations were usually short and caustic.

It was not long after the format change that I met with the general manager, Dick Casper and told him that I wanted to do a Sunday night talk show and talk about the Bible. The idea was to give Rogers and Cappas the option of telling callers to call Bill on Sunday night and talk about it. Bible talk was such a pressing issue that it went right to the top of the priority list. I think I met with Casper on a Thursday and his response was "Can you start this Sunday night?"

I had occasionally hosted a one hour talk show on a Christian station in Nashville a few years earlier, but this was different. WLAC covered 28 states after the sun went down and I had three hours on Sunday night to "do my thing!" I do, quite vividly remember the first few minutes of the first night on the air. The regular talk studio was still not ready so I sat down in a production studio with a microphone and a telephone and was cued that it was time for me to start talking. Needless to say I was praying as I spoke. It wasn't long before the calls started coming in and the fun had begun.

When vacation time came for the other hosts that next summer Dick Casper asked if I would fill in. By the end of the summer I was well versed in all of the shows. Then Charles Cappas became ill and left the station. That's when the regular weeknight edition of the Bill Steensland show started. I was still doing the Sunday night show for a while. We talked about the Bible on Sunday night and political issues the rest of the week.

From WLAC I moved to Memphis, Tennessee and was assigned the afternoon "Drive Time" slot on the WHBQ, which was the station that first played a recording by Elvis Presley! The next move was to Kansas City and KCMO.

In July of 1984 I left KCMO and moved to a family farm in Ohio. My wife Linda and I had five children at the time and the prospect of continuing to move around the country was almost certain. We made the decision that putting down roots in Ohio was more important for our children than having a well known and even well to do father. Now I'm not saying that I would have been either of those things had I stayed in the business but that was the direction I had wanted to go. I had been in Nashville, Memphis and Kansas City and the kids already showed some of the negative effects of moving. The children needed stability and even as a local host in Kansas City the death threats from "wacko's" were becoming too common. Then on June 18, 1984 Alan Berg was murdered in Denver. Alan was a pro Israeli talk show host at KOA and was murdered by some kind of white supremacists or Neo Nazis. I talked freely and often on my show of my support for Israel. The coverage of KCMO overlapped KOA and the manager of KCMO, who was incidentally Dick Casper, told me that it was time for me to get out of the controversial talk business. I don't know if he had received threats that made him come to that conclusion, but Dick never did anything without good reason. So we packed up and less than a month after Berg was killed we arrived in Ohio with two U-Hauls and five kids.

Why is Talk Radio so Popular!

There are two dynamics going on when you listen to a talk radio program. Either you are carrying on a "vicarious conversation" with the host, or you are peeping in the window of someone's soul as they bare it before all who would listen. In both situations you are captivated by what you hear.

The vicarious conversation is simple. The host makes a statement and then he articulates the response that is already in your head. After which, he responds again to you and then once again speaks the words you are thinking. In this case you are not listening to the radio; you are in a dialogue with the host. During this conversation if the host misrepresents your thinking you get the irresistible urge to call the show and straighten him or her out. The best callers are the ones who ring in to correct the host!

Looking in the window of someone's soul is fascinating. I would always know that I was getting there when my caller would say: "I never meant to say that on the radio." Hosting a talk show with callers is not the same as doing an interview. When you ask the questions in an interview your goal is to solicit all the pertinent information so the audience will understand the issue. With a caller however I most of all want his emotional posture to be exposed. And whether I agree or not, I want to provoke and poke so that we all can see the "true feelings" of the caller.

Many talk hosts today have adopted the "side kick" format. Instead of carrying on a vicarious conversation with the listeners the host can converse with the "side kick" and keep the words flowing nonstop. The dynamic between the host and side kick becomes the signature feature of the program. I'm sure the mother of the side kick loves it, but it definitely has less general audience appeal. You can go to any bar and hear this kind of banter. The side kick's real purpose is to keep the host from stumbling if there are no callers to the show. Except perhaps on the Glenn Beck program where Glenn and been a tremendous success doing exactly the thing that I have always thought was not the best way to do it! It just goes to show that there is always a great exception to the "rule."

I am not a sky diver, but I think hosting a talk radio show is somewhat the same. You step out of the plane as you intro the program and hope the parachute will open and save you from certain death. The callers are the parachute. How many times have you heard hosts begging for callers? If they don't call, the show crashes and burns! I learned that the way to get callers is to prepare not to need them! When I didn't need callers, they would call. When I felt like I needed them they were nowhere to be found. When the host has an "attitude" and communicates his "I know what you need to know and I know how you should live your life" perspective, callers will be lined up for hours to dispute his arrogance! I heard Rush the other day when a woman said "no one is perfect" he responded quietly "well there is one" and you could tell he was not talking about Jesus!

One personal tip is this: If you learn to be an accomplished talk show host, don't do it at home. Your wife and kids will not like it!

Civil Disobedience

According to the current Wikipedia definition, CIVIL DISOBEDIENCE is "the active, professed refusal to obey certain laws, demands, and commands of a government, or an occupying international power." The ONE THING that brought down Soviet control of Estonia, Latvia and Lithuania was singing. It has been called "The Singing Revolution."

"From 1987, a cycle of mass demonstrations featuring spontaneous singing eventually collected 300,000 Estonians in Tallinn to sing national songs and hymns that were strictly forbidden during the years of the Soviet occupations, as Estonian rock musicians played." (Source: Wikipedia "Singing Revolution")

Adam and Eve rebelled against God by eating the forbidden fruit. Righteous revolutions begin when men and women openly eat the "forbidden fruit" of a government by disobeying ungodly laws and regulations! Rebellious children do what their parents tell them not to do. A population can speak disapproval to the government and see nothing change, but when the people begin to engage in "civil disobedience," even if that disobedience is coming together to sing national songs and hymns the dynamic will shift!

Let me give you an example that never even seemed like it was a case of civil disobedience, but it clearly was. When Citizen's Band (CB) radios first came on the scene the government required that you purchase a license and that you use your call sign when using the radio. I did have a license, but I don't think I ever used the call sign, because no one else did.   There was massive civil disobedience when it came to CB radio licenses and using call signs.   The law was not enforced and the results were clear. The law passed away in 1983 because no one obeyed it! The protest against CB rules was not organized. There are no memorable leaders, but the impact was total.

What limitations of our freedom are being demanded by the government, but are certainly not founded in the Constitution? I think the most obvious one is the "separation of Church and State" myth.

One disadvantage of having your Bible on your smart phone, iphone, or ipad is that no one knows you are reading the Bible. You may think that is an advantage if you want to "stay out of trouble." But if you want to let it be known that you will not "honor" the unwritten rule that says you cannot read your Bible at school or in public it is much better to have a regular, leather covered copy of the Scriptures. Remember Daniel who, when he heard it was illegal to pray to God, went home and prayed in front of the window where everyone could see him. That bit of Civil Disobedience got him a full night in the lion's den.

Many people, even "good" people will say, "I don't want to be a trouble maker. So why do I want to stir things up when I can be quiet. I can be "religious" at home and be quiet about it when in public. Then no one will get mad."

We are all faced with a fundamental decision about accepting or rejecting the "status quo." If you accept how things are now and are not willing to help make positive changes in your life, community, country and yes even the world then you may eventually struggle with the "for what

purpose did I live" question.   When thousands of people

mailed TEA BAGS to Congress in 1982 they stood up and said

"I want things to be better!"

The End or the Beginning?

What must we do to keep from being enslaved by the rise of an oppressive government?

First of all, in your heart go to the Boston Harbor and dump the tea! Determine not to be ruled by dictators who give you no say in their new laws! Never agree to a law that has not been read by the people who vote for or against it!

Secondly, keep your eyes open and your ears alert for the coming of the ONE THING that will bring the American people together in voicing their concern for the centralized and pervasive corruption of our government. Recognize that it is only when we all speak at once, and speak the same thing that those in power will be unable to side step the protests!

Finally, recognize that the answer is God not Government. If we are not One Nation Under God, then we are a Divided Nation and Out of Control.

Today is either the time of the End of the United States of America or it is the beginning of a Rebirth of Freedom that will launch us into the future with amazing results! We can become an even greater nation of "God seekers" who build their world on His Word and His Will!

Determine that you will be part of the rebirth of the United States of America! May God bless you as you do and let the TEA BAGS RISE AGAIN!